THE WHOLE THING
THE REAL THING

brief biography of
SHRI GURUDEVA

Shri Jyotishpeethodwarak Brahmleen Jagadguru Bhagwan Shankaracharya Shrimad Swami Brahmanand Saraswatiji Maharaj of Jyotirmath, Badrikashram

English version by Prem C. Pasricha transcreated from the Hindi book by Rameswar Tiwari.

First Published in 1977
by
Delhi Photo Company,
New Delhi, India.

Printed at
Thomson Press (India) Limited
Faridabad, Haryana

ज्योतिर्मठ
पो० जोशीमठ
जि० चमोली

●

श्री बड़ानिवास
१७ भलोचीवहा
प्रयाग

●

बूरावाव
४२१०७

महात्माओं के जीवन चरित्र से सन्मार्ग प्रदर्शन हेतु सत्प्रेरणा प्राप्त
होती है । उनके अध्ययन से श्रद्धा बढ़ती है, भावना तथा निष्ठा दृढ़ होती
है । वह कागज पर नहीं, वरन् हृदय पर लिखने की वस्तु है । फिर भी भावी
पीढ़ियों के हितार्थ उसे लेख बद्ध करने की परिपाटी है ।

अखिल ज्योतिष्पीठाधीश्वर, परम पूज्य बाबा यै देव, की जीवन चरित्र
हिन्दी में प्राप्त है ही । अब श्री एफ ० वी ० पसरिचा, मालिक, देहली फोटो
कम्पनी, जनपथ, नई दिल्ली की प्रेरणा से उनके सुपुत्र श्री प्रेम ने उसे हिन्दीतर
भाषियों के लाभार्थ बाङ्गला भाषा में लिखने का प्रयास किया है, जो कि हिन्दी
मूल पर विशेषतःआधारित है ।

भाषान्तर में मूल भावों का यथारूप ठीक होना तो सम्भव नहीं है,
फिर भी यथा सम्भव श्री प्रेम ही पसरिचा के अपने प्रयास में सफल होवें इसी
हमारी मंगल कामना हेतु शुभाशीष है ।

शुभेच्छु
शान्तानन्द
सरस्वती

Preface

To the original Hindi Edition

How does one describe the Indescribable, circumscribe the Infinite, put into words That which is beyond all speech? This book is but an imperfect attempt to introduce to the eager and the devout an individual, who was an epitome of human perfection. Howsoever feeble this effort may be, its completion entails a feeling of total elation.

Pure, holy and luminous, whose very vision from afar bestowed peace, he was, to ascetics, an example of self-denial. Yogis saw him in union with the Divine. Sages found him calm, unruffled, wholly in tune with the cosmos. Paradoxically, he appeared withdrawn to the recluse, and full of involvement to the worldly.

Adorned in saffron silk robes, seated on a golden throne, he shone like the resplendent sun. Those around him sensed, as coming from him, rays of tender love, innocent simplicity, graceful compassion. Unconcerned about mundane matters, nevertheless, he brought into play his resolute will. Each word that he spoke was charged with a power that won the hearts of his listeners. Every person who came into his contact went away with the feeling of being the one who was closest to Maharaj Shri.

He was not in the habit of giving discourses. Whenever someone in a group used to ask him a question, he answered in such a way that others also felt their doubts dissipating. They reported later on that Shricharan had answered their questions without their having to utter them. His personality was replete with many such specialities for which ordinary explanations are inadequate.

In his elucidations, generally he used to relate his own experiences. This gave to his teachings a freshness that was irresistible to his audiences. It is because of this that we are able to have rare glimpses of his solitary life. This book, in fact, is mainly a collection of his life's experiences as narrated by him to his many devotees who took notes of what he said. Thus this biography can to an extent be described as an indirect autobiography. Truth-seekers are likely to find it beneficial.

Contents

SANTOSHI
KAVITA
SIYA
RAM
EKAATMATA
HUM
SHANTI

Shri Gurudeva *Shri Jyotish-peethodwarak Brahmleen Jagadguru Bhagwan Shankaracharya Shrimad Swami Brahmanand Saraswatiji Maharaj of Jyotirmath, Badrikashram*

CHAPTER ONE

The Child Ascetic

Glory to the Omnipresent, Omniscient, Omnipotent Supreme Soul who manifested Lord Rama in Ayodhya, a place that lies in the heart of what is now known as the state of Uttar Pradesh in Northern India. Glory to the One who brought forth Swami Brahmanand Saraswatiji Maharaj in the holy village of Gana, a place not far from Ayodhya.

Maharaj Shri was born on Thursday, December 21, 1870, in a Saryoopareen Panktipawan Gana Mishra Brahmin Zamindar family: highly respected, well-known, well-to-do. All the normal comforts and luxuries of life were available to him as a child. But who knew that he would one day spurn the velvet and prove himself a supreme ascetic yogi? And who knew that this yogi would one day grace the venerable seat of Shankaracharya?

Maharaj Shri's early years were very unusual. Even as a child he sensed the transitoriness of the world, and had an urge to renounce it. He was unconcerned about routine affairs. Loved solitude and mature behaviour. Disliked fickleness. His soulful transcendental look impressed everybody. He had no tongue for tasty sweetmeats nor an eye for fashionable clothes. He had no interest in the usual pleasures and entertainment, in toys and games that children play. He opposed purposeless talk and purposeless activity. Where he sat, he sat, lost in his own train of thoughts. Seeing his seriousness and unusually mature behaviour, family folks were astounded, and grasped, however vaguely, that they were in the presence of a celebrity in the making. Sharp intelligence, logical reasoning, quick decision-making: age, seven.

At that age he lost his most beloved companion, playmate, friend. His grandfather, a hundred years old, died. He was not allowed to see the corpse, though a servant took him to a window from where he managed to see the covered body of his grandfather being taken away to the chant of Ram Naam Satya hai, Ram Naam Satya hai, Ram Naam Satya hai.

Eyes closed as if in meditative sleep, his grandfather was going away forever, never to meet again, leaving behind his last message, 'Ram Naam Satya hai.' Lord, Thy Name is Truth. Lord, Thy Name is Truth. Lord, Thy Name is Truth.

The child's thoughts turned to Death. His grandfather, whom he had regarded as his own, had left. One by one, he thought, they would all leave: his father, his mother, his uncles and aunts, all his relatives. One day, he himself would be dead. When everyone has to go, no one is to live forever, then what is the truth? What is it that is permanent? What is it that will remain? Vibrating loudly in his ears was the sound, Ram Naam Satya hai—Lord, Thy Name is Truth.

Days passed, but the thoughts generated by this sound reverberated deeper and deeper in him. The sound was inerasably recorded in his innermost consciousness. It became the refrain of his life, his motto. He became more and more convinced about the illusion pertaining to this world. His folks, attributing his melancholy solely to his grandfather's death, wondered how to console him.

One year passed, he was eight years old. The Upnayan ceremony was duly performed in accordance with the Vedic rites. The sacred thread was put around his body. And he was sent to Kashi (Benares or Varanasi) for a study of the Vedas. As days passed, the cultural mainstream of the ancient city had a growing impact on him, so that he resolved that come what may, he would devote his life entirely to spiritual development.

The first test came soon enough. In accordance with the prevalent customs of high caste Brahmins in those days, his people now eagerly sought to get him married which, they thought, might also cure his other-worldliness. Relatives were sent to Benares to bring him back for this purpose. He who had not turned nine, not even shed all his milk-teeth was being told to get married. For most children, it is a time to wrestle and to play, to laugh and to romp about, but for him—marriage! Marriage and the incumbent wordly life, which he so much wanted to renounce, beckoned him. It was a major crisis for one so young in years but far advanced in intellect. He had to make a choice immediately between a life of sensual pleasures, of physical comforts, of luxuries, of satisfaction of normal human desires and a life of asceticism, of denial, of renunciation, founded on the permanence of Truth, promising peace and equanimity, and freedom from desire.

The path was chosen, the decision was made. The young ascetic in Kashi, renouncing all worldly desires, set out next morning on a lonely upstream journey along the banks of the river Bhagirathi (the Ganga). With his mind fixed on the inward Goal the child advanced in rapid steps alongside the Ganga. The sun rose, the sandy trail became hotter and hotter, but he kept walking, undeterred, calm, ready to face all challenges.

The river goddess suggested that he should drink a few sips of the holy water with the cup of his hands and rest a while under a shady tree. But he replied, "Mother, it is with your grace alone that I can make this long journey. Let me not get into the habit of stopping. Let me reach soon a cave in the Himalayas where I can sit and find my life's fulfilment." Saying this, he bowed to Goddess Bhagirathi and moved on.

Without rest, without sleep, unafraid of the desolate night, he moved on and on and on. On and on. On and on and on. Hungry or thirsty, or hungry and thirsty, he drank a few mouthfuls of the Ganga water with his hollowed palm, and moved on. On and on.

One day passed.

Two days.

What a test for Destiny to give to someone so young in years! And also to give him the fortitude that enabled him to pass it!

It was nearing sunset on the third day. The young traveller was moving onwards, kicking up a lot of dust, leaping over shrubs, when a zamindar (village landlord) noticed him and wondered who he was and where he was going. He tried to send for him through his servant, but could he dare do that and insult the young traveller moving so freely and with such single-minded intent? When the servant failed to elicit response, the zamindar went himself. "Who are you?" the zamindar asked, when he caught up to him at last.

Came the reply, "Why do you want to know? What is your intention?"

He entreated, "All I want to know is who are you and why are you going in such a great hurry on this rugged path at such an odd time."

The young ascetic said, "You are not in a position to know whether this is the right path or the wrong path, the right time or the wrong time. Sufficient for you to know that I am travelling from Kashi to the Himalayas in order to meditate. Go and mind your own business and don't trouble me for nothing."

The zamindar taken aback somewhat mustered courage

enough to say softly, "Maharaj, may I ask you when and where on the way you have begged for food?"

He got the reply, "So far the Ganga water has been my food and my drink."

"Then come and have some food and rest before going further. That will give me satisfaction. Moreover, it's getting to be dark."

"I'm not going to knock at anyone's door for food. As for satisfaction, I cannot believe that your giving me a meal would give you satisfaction. Satisfaction means that no desires remain and after that no desires arise. Your giving me alms is not going to give you that satisfaction. That can come only if you know the Supreme Essence, knowing which all else is known, and obtaining which nothing remains unobtainable. So make such efforts that bring you real satisfaction."

What a glorious philosophy from such an innocent mouth! The zamindar wondered about the extent of learning that must be in the institution that produced such talk from the lips of a mere youngster.

Milk was arranged on the river bank itself. Our philosopher friend poured two-thirds of it into the river as an offering in repayment of the water he had drunk during the last three days. The river goddess was immensely pleased and gave him a boon: He would never again need to quench his hunger with water alone. And indeed it so happened that during the many years that he spent in lonely caves or thick jungles or barren plains, he never had to beg for food and yet it came aplenty in some form or the other. Many a time on dark dismal nights in the forest, he would receive pots of cream and baskets of fruits from nowhere—from somewhere.

Onwards once again with the Himalayan journey to the Himalayas up the meandering bank of the Ganga. He said his evening prayers as was his daily practice.

When he felt hungry again, he ate some leaves or whatever he thought was edible, accessible. When he felt thirsty, he drank the holy water. When he felt tired, he slept, or rested under a shady tree.

The spiritual fire that burned within him gave his body a radiance and lustre that drew near him everyone who crossed his path. Some saw in him a modern Dhruva, some a modern Prahlad. (Dhruva and Prahlad were ancient Indian child saints.) A day passed. A night passed. The journey went on and on. After three more days, he noticed that the river had become very much broader. Actually he had arrived at the Sangam (confluence) of the rivers Ganga and Yamuna. He learnt from the people that he was in Prayag (Allahabad).

From his grandfather he had heard about the Triveni, or the sacred meeting-point of three rivers, Ganga, Yamuna and Saraswati. With great devotion he took dips at the holy spot. Then he moved onwards. Feeling tired, he sat down on a wooden plank near the riverside at the Dashashwamedh Ghat. Some time later, he was sitting, meditating, when a stranger came and sat down nearby. Both remained motionless for quite a long time. The stranger saw how different this child was from other children of his age. He looked tired and yet there was a glow on his face. The stranger took out a piece of paper from his pocket, read it, and looked again at the child's facial features. Then he came very close and sat down beside him. The child ascetic was shocked a little by this behaviour and looked curiously at him. The man once more took out the paper from his pocket and placed it before the child.

Child ascetic: What is this?
Man: Your description.
Child ascetic: Who are you?
Man: I am a policeman.
Child ascetic: What do you want?

Policeman: This is your description. You have run away from home....

Child ascetic: There is no need to talk much. It's just a description, isn't it?

Policeman: Yes.

Child ascetic: Then whoever has given you this description, inform him that I am here. If someone loses an animal, he reports a description to the police. But I am someone's son. Go and inform him that I have come here. If he wants he should take me from here.

Policeman: Yes, of course, I will inform. But tell me why have you come away from home?

Child ascetic: It's a fine question, "Why have you come away from home?" I ask you, why do you never leave your home?

For a while the policeman forgot who he was. He was wonderstruck by the philosophic logic of the little boy's retort.

Policeman: Everybody stays at home because that is where the comfort is. Why have you left the comfort of your home? Why are you wandering restlessly on the riverside on such a hot afternoon?

Child ascetic: Go, Sir, mind your own business. Go and enjoy the pleasures of home. In the lap of Mother Ganga, or on the sands, or walking on a silent afternoon in the wilderness—do I wander about restlessly or do I have the very bliss of life? —you'll never understand.

The policeman felt cut down to size, and sensed a great deal of respect for the child ascetic.

Policeman: You are young of age. But you seem to belong to a very high family. Roaming around like this—like an orphan—don't you feel...a-ashamed?

Child ascetic: It's true I'm small. But you consider yourself big, don't you? But being big you still don't understand who is an orphan and who is not an orphan. If you think

17

about it a little, then you will see that the Omnipresent, Omnipotent, Supreme Soul is everyone's Guardian, is everyone's Master, is everyone's Father. Whoever surrenders to Him, takes refuge in Him, puts himself in His protection, can he be regarded as an orphan? I ask you, whoever has not established contact with the Father, is he not an orphan?

Such sagacious words coming from the mouth of one so very young left the policeman speechless and he thought that this was no ordinary child but a Mahatma in the bud. After a few minutes' silence, the policeman said with great humility:

Now please do me a favour. Come with me because I have this description. I cannot actually leave you over here but I will not take you to the police station. You come with me to my house. You stay there the night. Tomorrow morning we'll do what we consider best.

After pleading with the child ascetic the policeman took him home. A long dialogue with the child during the night convinced the policeman that his hostage was bent upon reaching the Himalayas to devote his life exclusively to meditation with the sole objective of complete God-realization. The policeman thought that it would be better if the child could go by train. Early next morning the policeman made it clear that he did not want to be an impediment in the child's noble path. But his description had been relayed to police stations all over the country, and if he continued his journey on foot by the side of the Ganga he would get caught somewhere or the other.

What the child ascetic wanted now happened. He wanted to reach Haridwar the quickest possible way and now he was being requested to do so. What strange coincidence that the one who had come to obstruct him, wanted to help him to get away faster. Amazing indeed are the experiences of God's true devotees. The All-powerful, the

All-knowing God aware of the innermost desires of His seekers creates circumstances that bring about their fulfilment. The policeman bought him a ticket and put him on the train. Next day, the child ascetic reached Haridwar.

When he was going for a dip in the Ganga, a police inspector noticed him. The inspector saw that this was the same child for whom a big hunt was going on. "Why not send him home and earn a reward?" he thought, and with that followed him. Catching up, he asked, "Son, why have you left your home and where are you going?"

"In order to meet my Supreme Father I'm making straight for the Himalayas."

"I want to send you back to your people for which I'll get a reward."

"My decision is final. Even if you send me back, I shall not stay and will leave again the next day for this very place. So do not stand in my way and let me go. If, however, you are greedy for a reward, then do send me back and take your reward. Do as you like."

The police inspector was essentially a religious man. He heeded the child's request, and quietly went away.

Next day, however, as our young hero with Himalayan aspirations was moving towards Rishikesh, another police inspector accosted him. He also recognized him from the description available with him and remembered that there was a reward for tracing him. He was not to be persuaded and the child ascetic was sent back home.

CHAPTER TWO

Brahma Chaitanya
Brahmachari

On reaching home he tried to win over his elders to his ideas of world-renunciation and God-knowledge. They dismissed his talk as childhood obduracy. To the extent that he entreated them not to bind him to the materialistic life, they went ahead with matching speed to entwine him in wedlock. They were afraid that he might again slip out of their hands. On the child's side, however, was his unshakable faith and steadfast resolve. He stood firm on his earlier decision and totally refused to get himself hooked. It worried the elders very much, even though they realized that God willing, the elevated path which the child wanted to traverse would one day benefit not only him but the whole family, perhaps the whole world. But lifelong celibacy, the rigours and tribulations of the ascetic life and *at his tender age*—just this one thought was enough to make them shudder. They tried their level best to dissuade him but the young Mahatma was not to be swayed. Without God-perception, without intrinsic self-realization, was anything of any use?

The most highly respected man in the village, the guru of the family clan, was called. Panditji, experienced and learned, came, confident that he would be able to change the little boy's mind very easily, but all his erudition and diplomacy came to nought. Logic was met with logic, reason with reason. Panditji just couldn't win in his battle of wits with the young intellectual. Appealing to emotion, he said, "Son, you are the sole offspring of your parents.

All their hopes and aspirations are hinged on you. To serve them in their old age, it is your sacred duty. Don't leave them helpless and forlorn to spend the rest of their lives in darkness and sorrow. You are still a child. This is not the age to meditate in the jungles. Even if you have decided to renounce the world and practice ascetism, this is not the age to do so. First fulfil your filial responsibilities. Get married and obtain the experience of the worldly life. Then when the time is ripe, you can leave the humdrum and retire to the jungles. You will not be able to practise yoga properly if you go now with no experience whatsoever of the sensual life."

But who can *mis*lead one whom Destiny has chosen to rule over a spiritual realm? The reply came, full of confidence, "Panditji, your age is well nigh eighty, yet it's a matter of great regret that till now you have not had the desire to acquire knowledge of the Essence. It's a matter of shame that you are so much entangled in the worldly snare that you have not even thought of freeing yourself. If as a child it is my duty to stay at home, then as a grown-up you should depart to the jungle. I sense that I have reached the right decision and that it is my duty to go and that is why I insist on doing so. You had once said that the Scriptures say that even if one individual in the family attains to Truth-realization, the whole family is redeemed. If what is written is true then with Brahma-realization, I shall bring about the salvation of the whole family."

This sagacious reply had a salutary effect on the elderly priest who now relapsed into silence. Gradually, it dawned on him that the ignorant and upstart child whom he had been trying to reform was in reality a spiritual prodigy. Panditji called in all the members of the family to his side and said with intense religious feeling, "God has blessed your family with a saint child who shall bring great honour

21

to it." He stood up, folded his hands and bowed his head in veneration to the child Mahatma. Then, all of the members, young and old, turn by turn, did the same.

But the test was not yet over. Some people schemed that his mother be asked to press on the child to stay back on account of her love and attachment for him. Sitting behind a curtain, his mother listened to all this scheming. When some ladies actually put the idea before her, the child felt a little apprehensive because he did not want to be stopped by *her*. But the mother was in no way less broad-minded than her son. How could she thwart her son's quest for Supreme Knowledge? How could she act as a screen between her son and his bright golden future? She replied to the ladies, "Is it proper to stop someone who wants to devote himself to such a lofty search, to whom even our family guru has paid obeisance? Shall we take him down from the back of an elephant and set him up on a donkey? That he should forsake the path of salvation in order to enter the clap-trap life of a householder–I can never agree to that."

He asked his mother for permission to depart. "Go and sing in praise of the Lord," she said. "But remember, never to be a begging sadhu and if ever you miss the house-holder's life come back immediately."

Two days later he renounced his home, renounced his attachment to the illusory world, to his kith and kin, and set out in search of a place where he could meditate in solitude, away from the crowds, away from the noise, alone, entirely alone, face to face with Infinity, he and the Universe, beginningless, endless. One day he would strike a new path, give a new meaning, and start a new process which would eventually shape a new life-style for the people.

Reaching Prayag again, he had a bath at the Sangam. Finding a quiet spot on the sands, he sat down to meditate. For three days that was the unusual routine. Bath at the

Sangam and meditation. A policeman on the beat noticed the soulful child for three days and was amazed. On the third day, he approached the young meditator and asked him a simple question, "Maharaj, where are you coming from and where to do you intend to go?"

The answer was far from simple, "I have come from where the whole world has come, and I'm going to where the whole world is going."

"But you can't get on without money, can you?" the policeman tried again to communicate.

And failed. "My wealth is my destiny which is what I have accumulated since time immemorial. When that wealth is exhausted this body shall disappear and reappear no more. Please do not worry about me and get on with your job."

The policeman, already impressed by the shining face of the hallowed youngster and his upright demeanor, was so much moved by this little speech that he bowed to him with folded hands, and departed.

Destiny and faith shifted the scene to Haridwar. There also many religious-minded people, who go there for a holy dip in the Ganga, felt attracted towards this unusual child. But he ignored them as much as he could and remained busy with his hymns, prayers and meditations at an isolated spot, and then after a few days he trekked to Rishikesh.

Gateway to the Himalayas, Rishikesh is a scenic town situated at the foot of the mountains in a valley through which the Ganga flows. It has since ages been a place of great pilgrimage visited by seers and sages, yogis and ascetics, devotees of God and seekers of salvation. In the surrounding jungles, which are a visual treat, many aspirants find a secluded corner and practise according to their light and their Guru's instructions.

Reaching this place, the young aspirant felt that it would

be against the time-honoured tradition to practise entirely on his own. Even our divine incarnations and the great Shankaracharya had Gurus. So he must also search for his Guru and abide by his instructions. But who should be his Guru? Two qualifications he already knew. The Guru should be well-versed in the Vedas, and have knowledge of all the scriptures. He should be aware of the Immortal Self. To these two qualifications, he added two more of his own: he should be free from wrath and be a celibate since birth.

The search for the Guru began. Many names he had heard. He went and met them all. Some were learned pundits, some renunciates who had given up all their worldly possessions, some appeared to meet the first two qualifications but there were very few who met the most stringent one: lifelong celibacy. One staff-bearing Dandi Swami Mahatma was known to be a Bal Brahmachari and expert in the practice of Yoga. He was approached. Finding that he was immersed in Samadhi (intense meditation), our celibate celebrity-to-be waited outside. When Swamiji came out, his eyes sort of pinkish warm, with breathing exercises perhaps, he was greeted with great humility, "Om Namo Narayanaye (Let us bow to the Supreme Sustainer of the Universe). Some fire, my Sire, I require. Pray fulfil my desire."

Swamiji was incensed. Breathing fire and fury, he looked at him with bloodshot eyes and raged, "You fool, don't you know that Dandis don't keep fire? Asking me like that for fire ..." and he kept on raging.

"If you don't have fire, then where did all this come from," was the calm rejoinder from a few retreated steps.

That changed the air completely. Swamiji cooled down realizing the folly of his fiery histrionics. Feeling defeated he paced upto the little boy and hugged him and said, "Son, I feel sorry for having lost my balance. But, maybe,

Guruji of Shri Gurudeva
Disciple of Shringeripeeth,
Param Tapasvi, Bal Brahmachari,
Yogiraj, Dandi Sanyasi,
Shri Swami Krishnanand
Saraswatiji Maharaj of Uttarkashi.

it is in the nature of things for like poles to repel, and create a disturbance, though the pure Atman, the innermost individual Self, is without any turbulence. You are indeed great that at your age you have such a strong desire to light the inner fire."

"Swamiji, you have created such a stir and set me aflame."

"Great you are, great you are," said Swamiji. He praised the precocious 'fire-seeker', kept him in his Ashram for a few days and gave him a few lessons in Yoga. Swamiji would have liked him to stay on and most probably he would have, had Swamiji passed his third test, the test of even-temperedness.

The search went on, here, there, everywhere, through thick and thin, for the Guru who would measure upto his dreams. At last, he reached a place in the Himalayas called Uttarkashi. There he discovered a disciple of Shringeripeeth, Param Tapasvi, Bal Brahmachari, Yogiraj, Dandi Sanyasi, Shri Swami Krishnanand Saraswatiji Maharaj at whose feet he surrendered himself and received initiation and the name: Brahma Chaitanya Brahmachari, meaning literally, Truth-Conscious Celibate.

Swamiji was a master in Indian philosophy and yogic techniques. He was unequalled in his ability to translate the highest of ideals into the daily routine of life. Having attained to the Essence of Essences, he was indeed a living embodiment of Truth-Consciousness. In Swamiji's Ashram were many youths who had renounced their all and come with a fervent desire to realize God. He was satisfied with the earnestness and capability of the new entrant and would day by day enable him to be like himself: Self-complete, depleted of all egoistic desires, at peace with the world, one with One-Awareness.

There soon developed the most intimate connection between the Master and the disciple. The Master opened the floodgates of his limitless compassion and the disciple offered himself—completely—to the Master. This Master-disciple relationship has to be experienced to be fully appreciated. By and by, the hearts of Master and disciple vibrate so much in tune with each other that there remains not the faintest discord between the two. The disciple burning to ashes all his personal desires entrusts himself wholly to the Master. Focussing his attention on the expressed and unexpressed needs of the Master, he is ever alert to play his role in satisfying them. His thoughts are not his own; they are a reflection of his Guru's thoughts. His feelings are the feelings of his Guru. His total personality is merely a photostat copy of his Guru's personality. Having thus laid his all at the feet of the Guru, the *shishya* becomes a worthy claimant to the totality of his Guru's knowledge, to the entirety of his experience, to the bliss of His Being.

CHAPTER THREE

The Disciple

Once an eminent speaker in Indian philosophy paid a visit to Uttarkashi. He extended invitations to everyone interested to come and listen to his lecture. Guruji was also invited but he himself never used to go out anywhere. When his disciples expressed eagerness to hear the learned visitor and asked for permission, Guruji gave his consent. He told them to lock the Ashram gate from outside when they went, to keep the key with themselves, and on returning to open the lock and re-enter. When the time came for the speech, the Ashramites did as they were told. They locked the gate from outside and walked away without a second thought. His younger disciple, however, felt very uneasy. What sense did it make, he thought, to lock up their revered Guru who was a master among philosophers and, more than that, a knower of the Supreme Truth; to whom their all was surrendered and at whose feet lay their hopes of Integral Realization? To leave him, whose one word could spell salvation, and go to a bookish scholar who had the ability to speak fluently—was it really worth while? What could they expect to derive from listening to the orator that would absolve them of the crime of detaining their Guru under lock and key? Shameful indeed, it seemed. With each step his sense of guilt grew, so that finally the young disciple decided to retreat regardless of what the others did. But what reason should he give for returning? He did not feel it prudent to reveal his real thoughts as they might feel offended over his seeming impudence in thinking that he a newcomer was more devoted to Guruji than they who had already spent several years in the Ashram. So he said, "Since all the learned people in Uttarkashi are going to the lecture, I'm sure it's going to be a complex one with a lot of technical terms thrown in. Most probably, I won't understand it. I think it's useless for me to go. As such I might as well go back." Taking the key of the Ashram gate, he returned.

Nearing the gate he saw two Dandi Sanyasi Mahatmas advancing in the same direction. Hurriedly, he opened the gate, seated them in his small apartment and asked them whether they had had anything to eat. "It's with this intention that we came here while on our way to the lecture," said one of them. The young host quickly prepared some *halwa* for them. They ate it approvingly and left.

The young ascetic got busy with his routine. When in the evening the Ashramites returned from the lecture, the two Dandi Sanyasis were also with them. Guruji asked his guests whether they had had their repast. "Yes, Maharaj," they replied. "Right here in your Ashram before we went to the lecture."

"But this Ashram was locked? Where exactly over here?" queried Guruji.

The Sanyasis related the whole incidence. In conclusion, one said, "The young Brahmachari gave us a quick meal so that we got to the lecture in time."

When in the course of the daily routine, the young disciple went to pay obeisance to his Master, he was asked, "You didn't go to the lecture today?"

"No, Maharaj, I thought I wouldn't understand it, so I didn't go." When questioned about the Dandi Sanyasis he narrated the story as it took place. With his yogic perspicuity, Guruji sensed that there was much more to the episode than what appeared on the surface. He had fathomed the faith and devotion of his new disciple and seeing that it was deeper than that of all the rest, he now planned to fashion for him a special path for which his other disciples were not yet ready.

Next day, Guruji called his young disciple to his side and said, "You have acquired sufficient theoretical knowledge of the scriptures. The intellectual understanding so gained must now give way to actual experience which will come through the performance of certain yogic practices based on a special technique. This special technique, which I shall reveal to you, would, however, require that you stay all by yourself at another place away from the Ashram. Should you stay and practise here, my other disciples feeling jealous of you might hinder your progress. Some of them have been here for twenty-five years but lacking zealousness, they are not yet worthy claimants to the knowledge of this special technique. There is a place three miles away from here. You will go and stay there and practise this technique. Once every week you will come in the evening, spend the night in the Ashram and return early next day. Tomorrow, I will command you to leave for that place, but in order to keep your mission a secret, I will give you a big scolding in front of the others and tell you to pack up and leave the Ashram and go to that particular place. Don't be afraid of my scolding. Quietly collect your things and leave. Others will think that you have committed some blunder and incurred my displeasure. They will think I have banished you from the Ashram."

The young disciple expressed his total willingness to carry out his Guru's instructions. The special technique was clarified to him. Next day, as per script, Guruji created a dramatic scene in the Ashram. He appeared to be in a tempestuous mood, upbraiding all and sundry. When our hero appeared on the stage, others felt sheltered as he faced the torrent of words that were reserved for him. "Get out of here. This is no place for children. You have no business to be here. . . . Keeper, throw this little fellow out, get the hut vacated. And do it fast. . . . Get out."

"Where shall I go, Maharaj?"

"Go wherever you like. . . . Keeper, tell him about that place three miles away from here. If he wants he can go and stay there or he can go wherever he likes."

"As you please, Maharaj." The child ascetic bowed to Guruji, collected his belongings and seven days' food supply and made off to his new abode.

A week passed. Another week. Many weeks. Many, many weeks. Every Thursday, he visited the Ashram, laid himself at the Guru's feet, related his experiences and returned next morning with fresh instructions for the ensuing week. A new light dawned that grew brighter day by day, week by week, month by month, prodding him, guiding him, speeding him along the inward journey.

Guruji once sent a messenger to him to ask, "Is there any vacant place with you for me to come and stay?"

"No place at all," was the reply.

The devoted messenger taken aback pleaded, "One should be very careful about what to say to one's Guru. If I convey your reply to Guruji he will be even more displeased with you than he has been so far and he'd probably shift some of his displeasure on to us. I will tell him that there are a lot of rooms in the caves over there and that he's welcome to come and stay."

"Look here. I respect your age, your learning and your devotion to Guruji. Being elder to me, I honour you. But right now, you have come as a messenger. You have conveyed Guruji's question to me. Go and convey my answer to him: 'Not a single room over here is vacant.' After that whatever you like to say on your own, you may please do so. But my reply should reach him in my words: 'Not a single room over here is vacant.' If Guruji is displeased that will be my headache. You don't have to worry as you are just a messenger at present."

32

The messenger conveyed the reply. Guruji remained silent but the Ashramites were astounded at the insulting attitude of the young Brahmachari. He ought to be taught a lesson when he comes this Thursday, they thought.

Came Thursday evening. Came the Brahmachari to pay obeisance to his Guru. All the Ashramites looked askance at him and waited eagerly to see what chastisement was in store for him at the hands of Guruji. When Guruji remained calm and quiet, one of the disciples, who thought himself to be extra close to the Master, said, "Maharaj, what penance, what atonement is prescribed for a person who disrespects his Guru. Disrespect amounts to contempt, does it not? How should such a man be treated who disrespects his Guru, shows contempt for him?"

Guruji, well aware of the Ashramites' mood, posed innocence, and said: "Your question is not yet very clear. Why don't you illustrate it with an example?"

The questioner hesitated but, seeing no way out, went on: "That day, Maharaj, you had expressed a desire to go and stay in one of the rooms in the caves where the young Brahmachari is staying. You sent a messenger to enquire whether there was room over there and the messenger returned with the curt reply that there was no room available there, whereas the fact is that many rooms were and still are lying vacant over there. This insulting attitude has hurt all of us very much and we would like you to tell us how we should behave towards this impertinent young fellow."

Guruji turned his face towards the young Brahmachari and queried, "Well, what have you to say in this connection?"

"Shricharan, you alone are fit to guide my fellow disciples as regards how they should behave towards me. As for what I said that day, it was absolutely true and it is still true that there is no vacant place with me whatsoever."

Voices intervened, "What about two rooms in the corner . . . ?" "What about the rooms facing your room?"

"Do I not know the correct position?" murmured the Brahmachari.

Guruji intervened, "Why don't you make everything clear to them?"

"Maharaj, it's a matter between you and me. They are in no way concerned and. . . . "

"All right. All right. You explain yourself to me. If they want to listen, let them do so."

The young Brahmachari clarified himself thus: "As far as I've been able to understand, Guruji, you do not live in houses made of stone and clay. You live subtly in the hearts of your devotees. Shricharan, all the space in my heart is already occupied by you. The day I surrendered myself to you, I emptied every nook and corner of my heart and filled it up with love of you. No room lies vacant in here. As for the rooms in the caves where I live, Maharaj, you already know that they are lying vacant and had you desired to stay in one of them, you would have done so without your asking me. Who am I to ask, anyway? I took it, Maharaj, that you wanted to know about the rooms in my heart and it is in that context that I gave the reply that all the rooms were full and not a single one is vacant." After saying this, the Brahmachari took a deep breath and lapsed into silence. His face reddened. He looked awkward and embarrassed as if he had been made to strip. The great grand secret which he had treasured all this time now lay bare before banal eyes. He wished he had not been called upon to express the mystery of his unquestioning faith, his unalloyed devotion, his unadulterated love, his impassionate self-surrender to his Guru.

It came as a revelation to his other disciples. They looked at each other and buried their eyes in shame. What they had mistaken for a small piece of coal was really a big sparkling diamond with just a thin veil of coal-dust on it. Whom they had thought to be an arrogant fool turned out to be a humble sage. They regretted their shortsightedness and their eyes were filled with moist repentance.

Guruji's eyes were also liquid with love. The secret of the great romance between the Master and the disciple was out at last. It was a profound moment of truth that stretched itself into an hour having the appearance of Eternity. The deep silence was broken at last by Guruji, "All of you please leave." One by one the disciples retired to their huts except the Brahmachari.

"Forgive me for having expressed my treasured secret love for you," he said.

"It's true that this is a very personal matter," said Guruji. "But what has happened has happened well. Think no more about it. What you have done was at my behest. Love, faith, surrender form the basis of all inner development. But can they be taken away from you and shared, or even emulated? Hardly. That is the law of nature!"

CHAPTER FOUR

The Recluse

Twenty-five was the age when Shri Maharaj accompanied by his Guruji descended from Uttarkashi having completed his study of the scriptures and having discovered the truth about his innermost Self. For about a month, they stopped over at the small picturesque village of Kajliwan, near Rishikesh. Set amidst a dense jungle that supported many wild carnivorous animals, it was a place that nevertheless held a special welcome to the Sadhus and Mahatmas. Maharaj Shri and Guruji were given a rousing reception by the people of Kajliwan and other surrounding villages.

Among the throng of darshan-seekers was a Brahmin milkman, whose practice it was to offer milk to the holy guests that visited the place. Maharaj Shri arranged with him to bring everyday half a litre of milk which he would boil and serve to Guruji every night. One day, it so happened that the Brahmin's wife said, "The cow has given very little milk today. It will not be enough even for the children."

The Brahmin, however, paid no heed to his wife and supplied half a litre as usual to the honoured guests. When Maharaj Shri warmed up the milk and served it to Guruji, he said, "There is woe in the milk today. I shall not drink it. Please return it to the milkman and tell him to stop giving it." Maharaj Shri did as he was told. About fifteen days later, as fate would have it, the milkman's son died. The whole place was agog with the rumour that Guruji was displeased with the Brahmin milkman and therefore he had lost his son. Maharaj Shri conveyed this to Guruji, who merely said, "When the people take the boy's corpse to the cremation grounds tell them to send for me before making the funeral pyre."

That was done. The corpse was placed on the ground pending Guruji's arrival. Guruji came. He had the strings securing the shroud removed and kicked the lifeless head gently with his foot, saying, "Why do you sleep so much?" And lo, the boy was on his feet! It was a miracle that dazed everyone present. Wonderstruck, they bowed to the great Mahatma in their midst.

On reaching their hut, Guruji said to Maharaj Shri, "It's better to leave this place right now before all the dead people here start pestering us for life!" And with that Guruji left—leaving Maharaj Shri alone!

*   *   *

The Ganga was in furious flood, rising every minute. All the low lying spots threatened by the gushing waters had already been vacated. But two Sadhus, caring two hoots about their safety, continued to sit calmly on their wooden planks that were tied by ropes to two separate acacia trees. Maharaj Shri saw them and wondered why they were so unconcerned about their lives when they could, like the other Sadhus, have easily found shelter elsewhere. In order to probe their fate, he climbed up a tree situated at a higher point and kept a constant vigil on the Sadhus. Three days thus passed but the three of them remained rooted to their precarious spots, unmindful of the danger. On the fourth day, the torrential flow of the flooded Ganga uprooted one of the acacia trees and set it afloat. The wooden plank tied to it, with the Sadhu still sitting on it, was also afloat! But what did Maharaj see? Not the least trace of worry on the floating Sadhu's face. No anxiety. No perplexity. Calm, composed, unperturbed he gave a beaming smile to the other Sadhu, "Glory to the Lord of the Universe. At last, I'm on the move." The other one unmoved by the situation returned the smile and said, "Glory to the Lord of the Universe. Wherever you be, in whatever circumstances, remember Him and remain steadfast."

It was an unforgettable spectacle for Maharaj Shri to see the Sadhu being carried speedily down the river by the swift current and after covering a distance being landed safely and emerging unexcited, tranquil, serene, placid, as if unaware of everything except the glory of God.

* * *

A prosperous businessman of Calcutta used to visit Rishikesh every winter and distribute shawls among the religious fraternity. Seeing Maharaj Shri, scantily clad, sitting in the open and meditating in the biting wintry wind, he wrapped a shawl around him and sat down facing him. When after a while Maharaj Shri opened his eyes he saw the wealthy merchant sitting in front of him, and asked him, "Why have you put this shawl around me? What do you want? If you have done this in charity thinking me to be a mendicant, you have not done a proper thing, for no true Sadhu or Mahatma is a poor man. If, however, your intentions are different, pray tell me what they are."

The rich man bowed and said meekly, "My Lord, I am a Marwari trader. I have heard learned men quote the scriptures that whoever gives away one rupee in charity to a Mahatma gets a thousand rupees in return. I have donated one shawl to you in the hope that with your blessings I will get a thousand in return."

Maharaj Shri calmly unwrapped the shawl from his body, folded it carefully and returned it, saying, "Here take one right now, I will try and arrange for the remaining nine hundred and ninety-nine." Sethji was taken aback and felt afraid for having offended the Mahatma. He was too numbed even to make a proper apology. Maharaj Shri, however, put him at ease. "Just tell me if you could possess all the world's wealth, all the property, all the world's comforts and luxuries, would you be able to use them all? One day, you'll have to leave everything here. By the grace of God, you are already enjoying enormous wealth and even have the opportunity to give away a part of it, at least, in charity. But still you are greedy for more. How will it benefit you in the long run if all your attention is fixed on just greater and greater material prosperity?"

Sethji was suitably impressed by Maharaj Shri's response to his 'investment gimmick', and went away figuring out the true meaning of charity. Give, give, till it hurts.

*　　*　　*

Maharaj Shri was on pilgrimage to Badrinarayan alongwith three other Brahmacharis. On the way, he said, "As a rule I never keep any money with me. Since we are travelling together, I suggest that if any one of you has got any money with him, he should either leave it at some place or he should leave this company. Otherwise there's bound to be trouble. The one with money may not be able to use it the way he wants to if he remains with us and thus his psychic vibrations may not be in tune with that of the group. It's better that either he leaves us or at least his money leaves us."

One of the Brahmacharis said, "I have three sovereigns with me which are at your disposal. I do not want to break away from you all in any case." It was decided to bury the three gold coins under a particular tree and to retrieve them on the return journey. The money was buried and the four Brahmacharis got on with the pilgrimage.

As destiny would have it, one week later, the moneyed

Brahmachari, exhausted with the mountainous travel, fell prey to a poisonous infection and died. His last rites were dutifully performed and the remaining three Brahmacharis proceeded sedately with the journey to Badrinarayan. The pilgrimage over, they returned to the spot where the lucre was buried. Maharaj Shri suggested that they dig it out and give it away in appropriate charity. But when they dug the particular spot, they found a thin snake, coiled around the gold sovereigns, having a colour that was almost indistinguishable from the treasure that it guarded.

Maharaj Shri said, "It is written in the Vedas that if the last thoughts of a dying man are on his buried wealth, he will have to be reborn as a snake. This is evidently a proof of that statement. It appears that during his last moments, the Brahmachari's thoughts were wrapped around these sovereigns." Maharaj Shri took hold of the serpent and flung it into the Ganga flowing nearby. The Brahmachari got a quick deliverance from his serpent incarnation. His sovereigns were later given away in charity, aiding him further perhaps in his journey through countless births to the Badrinarayan situated in the innermost recesses of his spiritual heart.

*　　*　　*

A great debate went on in Prayag between some fishermen and their detractors. Maharaj Shri was called upon to decide the issue. When they came to him he said, "Please come tomorrow morning."

The next morning the fishermen cast their nets as usual before calling on Maharaj Shri. The detractors protested. Maharaj Shri asked the detractors to bring him six or seven pebbles the size of a gram grain. When these were brought, he handed them back to the detractors saying, "Now go and throw them in the places where the fishermen have cast their nets and all of you come back in the late evening."

There was great jubilation among the detractors when they returned to see Maharaj Shri in the evening. Not a single fish had been caught. The fishermen simply did not know what to make of this remarkable occurrence. They simply bowed in silence to the Mahatma and went away.

*　　*　　*

Years that passed must have been replete with many interesting and educative incidences but we know not the details. His consecrated life, never deficient, had no need to keep a record of itself. His Guru's grace had bestowed on him many special qualities, many extra-ordinary powers. Always busy in deep Self-meditation in lonely wilderness or in dense forests that provided him the company of lions and tigers, elephants and antelopes. Food there was aplenty: seeds, weeds, roots, fruits. He never asked for alms. Charity he did not accept. Aloof from society, away from the wiles of women, untainted by monetary considerations, he lived these years as a child in the lap of mother nature whose face was Kashmir, whose breasts were Gangotri and Jumnotri, and whose body was the many mountains, forests and jungles of the Indian subcontinent.

CHAPTER FIVE

Shri Swami Brahmanand Saraswati Maharaj

At the age of thirty-six, on the occasion of the auspicious Kumbh fair at Prayag, Guruji's illustrious disciple was formally ordained into the ascetic order. Guruji presented him with a kamandalu (a kettle-shaped wooden pot) and a kaupeen (a brief lioncloth) and gave him the name, "Shri Swami Brahmanand Saraswati Maharaj."

The Vedic ritual was performed at the holy confluence, Triveni Sangam, in the presence of a large gathering of Brahmacharis, Sadhus and Dandi Swamis. They were given a sumptuous feast and honoured with many presents.

Maharaj Shri, already much sought after for his darshan and blessings, was even more sought after now. He still preferred to live a secluded life but whenever he visited places such as Kashi, Prayag and Ayodhya, people got wind of his presence and thronged his abode for his darshan. His devotee hosts, aware of his love of solitude, usually made arrangements in the upper portion of their buildings, where he could and did shut himself up for long stretches of time. It was not impossible to have his darshan but it was certainly very difficult. People used to start collecting from 4 p.m. onwards and would wait for his darshan fixed from 8.30 p.m. to 9.00 p.m. He would ask for a list of the people waiting for his darshan, study it, and on many days, at nine, he would send a message to the darshan-seekers, "Will not meet today." In fact, he had got a sign-board prepared in Hindi which conveyed this message, "Aaj nahin milenge." Many people with disappointment writ large on their faces would reluctantly leave the place to try their luck on another day. Sometimes, after about two hours, he would enquire whether any of them had stayed on. On getting a positive answer such as, "Two persons", he would say, "Please ask them to come up."

When they came, he would make much of them and say, "These are the genuine seekers, others were just casual visitors." He would have a hearty talk with them and relate his experiences with great gusto that served to illustrate his philosophy and ethics. He would usually pass on to them a treasure key that helped them later to resolve their problems and enrich their lives. They would go thanking their stars for having risked the extra wait.

CHAPTER SIX

The Master

Held every twelve years, it was the Kumbh fair once again at Prayag, in 1930. Arrangements for Maharaj Shri's stay at Daraganj had already been made by one of his affluent devotees, one Mr. Tiwari. Ten rooms were lying vacant eagerly waiting to be filled by his benign presence. At the last minute came the message that Maharaj Shri would avoid the swarming Kumbh multitudes at Prayag and had already gone to stay in a cell in the Temple of Mahadev on the banks of the Ganga at Kaureshwar, a quiet place twelve miles to the west. His disciples, some Dandi Sanyasis, the message added, would however be utilizing the rooms reserved for him during the period of the Kumbh. Though disappointed over the change in programme, Tiwari consoled himself by giving a proper welcome to Maharaj Shri's disciples. Hardly had he done so, when he was put to a severe test. An important business friend of Calcutta requested Tiwari to accommodate in his Daraganj mansion his family folks who were keen on seeing the Prayag Kumbh. Tiwari did not say no to the Calcutta Seth and requested Maharaj Shri who had chosen not to grace his premises to ask his Dandi Sanyasis to vacate the rooms in favour of his rich friend's family. Maharaj Shri replied, "Since you had earlier extended a warm welcome to my disciples, it would not be advisable to turn them out now and insult them. I suggest you make an alternative arrangement for Sethji's family."

Tiwari felt rebuffed and even thought of using force against the innocent Sanyasis but Maharaj Shri saw to it that he did not succeed in his vile attempt—or rather that he did not fail to pass in the divine test. As a friend, one could count on Maharaj Shri's grace; as a foe, one could count on his grace marks!

*   *   *

A humble devotee of Maharaj Shri, one Mr. Kuberdutt Ojha, was a resident of Daraganj, Prayag. When he learnt about Maharaj Shri's stay at Kaureshwar, he cycled all the way daily after office hours for his darshan. It so happened that Maharaj Shri's Guruji also came to Prayag in those days and chanced to stay at Ganga Bhavan, situated in the same Daraganj locality. Kuberdutt used to visit both the Mahatmas everyday and became a sort of messenger between them. Guruji enquired whether Maharaj Shri would be visiting Prayag during the Kumbh.

Came the answer, "No likelihood."

Guruji's comments on this answer were relayed to Maharaj Shri that evening.

"What!" exclaimed Maharaj Shri. "He says it doesn't matter if I'm not going to Prayag. He will come and meet me here. Good God, *he* will come and meet *me* here. Kuberdutt, go right now and make arrangements for a motor to pick me up at 4 a.m. so that I get to Daraganj before sunrise tomorrow."

Kuberdutt complied with Maharaj Shri's request that sounded like a humble entreaty. A car was brought and very soon Maharaj Shri found himself face to face with his revered Guru. He was about to prostrate himself on the ground in the usual manner but Guruji took him into his arms and embraced him. He made him sit next to him on his dais and muffled his loving protests, saying, "Come, come, sit down. It's proper. It's proper."

About a hundred persons who were gathered there witnessed this unusual drama when Master and disciple were out to outdo each other in their expression of affection. When the supreme state is reached, who is the Master, who the disciple?

"You have spent enough of your lifetime in forests and mountains," said Guruji. "Now spend more of your time in towns and cities so that people can derive the benefit of your vast learning. As it is, you are unmatched in answering questions and clearing the doubts of the people."

* * *

Maharaj Shri was under attack. A Sadhu-looking man was calling him names, loudly criticizing him, and uttering a lot of obscenities. The Ashram people tried to pacify the intruder but since it only made him more vituperative, they were about to give him a good thrashing, when Maharaj Shri intervened. He called them aside and said, "I have given you many lessons on big and small matters, but so far I have not been able to give you a lesson in tolerating intolerance. God has today given me an opportunity to give you that lesson. Try to remain calm while this man hurls abuses at me."

One Brahmachari said, "Forgive me, but the prime law-giver Manu had ordained that no one should in any case listen to the criticism of one's Guru."

"Right, right, the idea being not to think ill of one's Guru. But at the moment I want you to ponder over the question: Is it harmful to be criticized? Or is it beneficial? If you believe in Destiny, what will be, will be, success or failure, happiness or sorrow—not one whit can be changed by anyone's criticism. So you might as well ignore it. Scriptural pundits, in fact, opine that critics help to wash away the sins of the sages, and are really more of an aid to their spiritual development. Many saints treat their most vociferous critics at par with their most

46

devoted followers. The devotees serve and worship the Mahatmas but share with them their hoard of spiritual powers, but the critics take nothing for themselves, they just wash away their sins. We should indeed be very grateful for the beneficial service that they render and should in no case try to stifle their criticism."

The Ashramites, thus subdued, listened quietly to the mock Sadhu's tirade which went on unabated for well over an hour. After that he sat down to rest for a while under a shady tree. Shri Charan invited him and said, "Friend you must be tired. Allow us to serve you some refreshments."

Maharaj Shri's critic-guest was given a good feast by the Ashramites. When he stood up to go, he was given two rupees on his host's bidding. These were to enable him to go by horse carriage. It was learnt later that when he joined his comrades, he expressed remorse over his unseemly behaviour and had nothing but praise for Maharaj Shri, which he openly sloganized the next day in the Ashram, "Swamiji ki jai ho! Swamiji ki jai ho! Glory to the Master! Glory to the Master!"

* * *

Maharaj Shri was in Prayag staying at the posh bungalow of Raja Dhingvas. Close by lived an advocate devotee, who had heard that Maharaj Shri remained awake the whole night singing hymns. Feeling rather inquisitive, one day he entreated, "Maharaj, I have heard that you sit through the night, pray and meditate and sing praises of the Lord. Please allow me to witness this at least once."

Maharaj Shri smiled, "Will you be able to stay awake for one full night?"

"Yes, I'll try my best," replied the advocate.

"Okay. It doesn't affect me in the least, but be careful. Not a word about it to anyone."

But the word spread that the advocate had spent a night with Maharaj Shri! Some inimical scandal-mongers, tasting blood, plotted a strategem to drag the saint into the mire. They got hold of a call-girl, bribed her heavily, dressed her up as a man and made her join the darshan-seeking throng. After the others left she was to keep Maharaj Shri's company on some pretext or the other and try to seduce him to a lustful night with her. When the time came for her to act, she lost her nerve, or God knows what happened, but she let out an eerie scream and ran down the steps. The conspirators waiting downstairs enquired what she was up to. "Ooh! My body—it's aching all over. Ooh! Why did I ever listen to you?....He's a saint. He's a saint."

Does a saint discriminate between a man and a woman, between one man and another? Perhaps, one has to be a saint to judge a saint. Anyway, self-committed as a Brahmachari to remain untouched by women, he had issued strict instructions prohibiting the entry of women (and untouchables!) to his dwelling place in the Ashram. If they wanted to bow to him or to have his darshan, they could do so at the Ashram gate whenever he passed through it, going out or coming in.

Once in Prayag, he was staying in a house situated on the banks of the Ganga. He received a request to see him at his place from a widow belonging to the esteemed family of Pandit Madan Mohan Malaviya, who was one of India's foremost freedom-fighters. As per his rule, the request was turned down. She, a learned lady, who loved the company of devout people, wrote a note to him, and demanded an explanation. He who was born of a woman, whom he probably loved very much, why did he now treat women at par with untouchables? Maharaj Shri put her off for a day or two but when she insisted through a messenger for an immediate reply, he wrote:

"I spent nine months in intimate contact with you womenfolk. How shabbily was I treated! Hung upside down in solitary confinement in a dark, damp, dingy cell—I can never forget those days. That is the reason why I have lost all desire for your company.

"The potter moulds a water pot, gives birth to it. The water pot finds its way to the Holy sacrarium. But the potter stands outside, not permitted to enter the Sanctum."

The lady read the letter and went about checking on Maharaj Shri's daily routine, and his programme during the next few days. Next morning at 4 a.m. he left by boat for the Sangam and was having his dip at the holy Ganga confluence when a blissful female emerged from the water and said with glee: "Here everyone has the right to your darshan!"

*　　*　　*

A rich Calcutta merchant used to visit Prayag frequently in connection with a case in the High Court. Sometimes, when he went for a bath in the Ganga, he also paid a visit to Maharaj Shri staying in Daraganj. Maharaj Shri's magnetic personality whetted his appetite— a very common occurrence—so that he came more and more often seeking his darshan. Sethji told him about his lawsuit in the High Court and hoped that with his blessings it would be settled in his favour. Maharaj Shri listened to him but maintained a vibrant silence. However, as it usually happened with such supplicants, Sethji won.

In India people often make their offerings in a dona (pronounced though-na), which is made of dry leaves folded up in the form of a cup. Jubilant over his victory, when Sethji went for the next darshan, he took with him a dona. The dona was filled with sovereigns which were concealed under a layer of fragrant jasmine flowers. He placed the dona near Maharaj Shri's feet and prostrated himself before him. The religious communion went on till late in the night when Sethji and all other visitors left for their homes and Maharaj Shri retired to his private room. Next morning, the Brahmachari attendant while cleaning up the place discovered the sovereign-filled dona and brought it to the Master's notice. Maharaj Shri immediately issued instructions that should Sethji come for his darshan in the evening, he should be stopped at the gate and not allowed to enter without his specific permission. Sethji when he came that evening was shocked when he was made to wait at the gate for an excruciating two and a half hours, before he could be allowed in and have Maharaj Shri's darshan.

"You make an offering of sovereigns to us, do you? To those who desire them, to them you do not give. To those who ask for them, to them you do not give. Then why do you give them to us? Do I need them to marry off a son or a daughter? . . . Go, take these, and give them to those who crave for money." Maharaj Shri returned the sovereigns and added, "We don't need your money here. If you have to make an offering, offer not your money but your defects, so that you are redeemed and are made whole."

* * *

Where do we go from here, we do not know. But Maharaj Shri went wherever his footsteps took him. And usually, they took him in straight lines. Stepping across ditches, jumping over hurdles, trespassing fields, it was not for him to keep on man-made roads and stick to pedestrian routes!

Sometimes, he would get a shout, "Hey! Keep off my field. Go by the proper path."

He would reply, "Forgive me, sir, for my poor road sense. But I have always travelled by the straight path of renunciation and do not know how to go over the smooth curves of materialism."

50

There were other occasions when instead of receiving an admonition, he would be trailed by a crowd of devotees. Once, being aware of a commotion behind him, he looked back and saw people picking up something from his track, and enquired, "What are those people doing?"

"They are collecting dust from the places where your feet have touched the ground." That was finite movement par excellence wholly in step with the Infinite.

*   *   *

Wandering about he reached a village near Manikpur. His hallowed appearance immediately attracted the villagers' attention and evoked their warmest hospitality. "Is there any secluded place around these parts where I can meditate in silence and solitude?" he asked.

Yes, there was a cave about five miles away, the people told him. But it was situated in a dense jungle infested with wild animals. And, what is more, they related a story to him regarding the cave:

Once the son of the village zamindar was moved by the spirit of renunciation. He asked his henchmen to take guns and escort him safely to the cave. When they got to the cave, he went inside and ordered the others to return home. They, however, settled down under a bush nearby and decided to spend the night there. At night, they heard weird feminine peals of laughter emerging from the cave. There were sounds of slapping and of something pounding the walls of the cave. None dared to enter during the gruesome night. Next morning they went in and found the boy lying in a stupor with blood hand-prints all over his body. They lifted his unconscious body and brought him home.

"Let it be seen," muttered Maharaj Shri, and after a while without saying anything to anyone walked off in the direction of the cave. The five miles he covered in two hours. He looked around and saw it was a fascinating spot where he could carry on his romance with himself.

51

He settled down under a tree, fully poised and totally unafraid.

Came night as dark as soot. But, what, suddenly it was light as bright as day. The forest vegetation upto a quarter of a mile glowed in the supernatural illumination. Still calm and unexcited, he drew a small circle around his seat, and waited. Slowly the colour of the light changed and it turned to a flashy fluorescent blue. He saw moving about sages belonging to a distant era. Now there was the image of Rama, Laxmana, Sita in the forest. Now, the child Krishna with his alluring smile. And then after half-an-hour of what can be called a fantastic multi-dimensional movie, it was darkness once again. Nimbus clouds gathered overhead. It thundered. It rained. Hailstones fell from the sky. And bones. And blood. Maharaj Shri sat quietly, safely inside his little fortress, witnessing these queer dreamy happenings.

Seeing that his superscope extravaganza had not made the slightest impact on his one-Mahatma audience, the producer-director of the show now emerged from behind the screen. He came sitting on a lion and asked, "Who are you and why have you come here?"

Maharaj Shri saw before him a giant of a man. Tresses of his matted hair grazed the ground. His eyes were half-hidden behind his big bushy eyebrows. Maharaj Shri gave him a smile and countered his question, "To whom were you showing this little play of yours?"

He, an Aghori Mahatma, a sort of a sorcerer-sage, now on the defensive said rather meekly, "Should you need anything over here, pray tell me. I can immediately get you whatever you want. But please at least introduce yourself."

Came the reply, "Surely, if you are capable enough to fulfil my desires, you ought to be able to find out who I am and why I have come here. I do not desire anything.

By the grace of the Guru, I am perfectly satisfied." Aghori's insistence that Maharaj Shri should ask him for something only evoked the questions, "Have you come here to tempt me? Do you want to degrade me?"

The Aghori, now fully convinced that here was someone whose treasures surpassed his own, said, "Forgive me. I have behaved naughtily. But you are the first man who has stood his ground before me. I have not met anyone so richly endowed as you are, during the two hundred and fifty years I have spent in this jungle. Please forgive me." He paused for a while, then added, "Please stay here as long as you like. And should you find me fit to serve you in any way, please ... please don't hesitate ..."

Maharaj Shri reiterated that all his needs were being fully met. He had come awandering, awandering he would go. And so it was. He left the place a few days later so that the Aghori could continue, unhampered, with the production of his make-believe drama, which probably held him spell-bound!

*　　*　　*

Walking on a bridle path in the thick jungle, he saw a lion standing at a distance blocking the path. Unconcerned, he advanced in merry steps. Nearing him, he addressed him as one God's creature to another, "It's not in the fitness of things for a king to stand in the way of other people." The lion wagged his tail in acknowledgement and moved to one side, letting, perhaps, a bigger lion to pass.

*　　*　　*

During the course of his travels, Maharaj Shri came across a magnificent banyan tree. Just by the side of the tree was a steep cliff that seemed to be the only access to a breathtakingly beautiful basin down below replete with a crystalline water-spring. Our Tarzan friend clutched the sinewy banyan branches at hand and blissfully descended into the abyss, shall we say. Beside the spring he discovered a cave exquisitely designed by the Supreme Architect. For food, he found an underground hoard of sweet potatoes.

A millionaire could not have afforded such luxury, but Maharaj Shri was more than even a multi-millionaire. He stayed in great style in this palatial Garden of Eden that had evidently been specially constructed for him. He stayed there like an aristocratic Adam for many, many months.

India in those days was ruled by the British, who had a penchant for big-game hunting. Finding Maharaj Shri's 'estate' suitable for such sport, an Englishman made arrangements for a lion-hunt. The villagers brought a buffalo for a bait, tethered it securely near the spring, and went away. The hunter located a vantage point quite some distance away and waited with his men for his quarry. The buffalo, struggling furiously to set itself free, got injured, and bellowed with pain and continued to do so for many hours. Maharaj Shri listening to the piteous animal cry went out in the dead of the night to investigate and saw what was up. He placed the tough rope over a big stone and mashed it with another stone till it was cut asunder. The buffalo scampered away and Maharaj Shri returned to his meditation cave.

At dawn, after a night's enervating vigil, the hunting party came and discovered to their chagrin that someone had severed the rope and set the buffalo free. The irate Englishman voiced a lot of obscenities. The God-fearing villagers tried to pacify him saying, "There is a Mahatma living here in these parts who has probably done this. It is not proper to speak ill of him."

"What Mahatma!" burst the Englishman's proud wife,

who had just joined the group. "How dare he do this to us. Who is he anyway to spoil our sport? We are the rulers of this land. This land belongs to us. This jungle belongs to us. We will do what we like. Tell your Mahatma to mind his own business or else ... " Hardly had she finished her little speech, when she felt a shooting pain in her stomach. It so happened that her excretory functions came to a dead stop. Her torso swelled alarmingly.

The villagers advised the Englishman to trace the Mahatma and request him to cure his wife. After a brief combing operation, the lion-hearted Mahatma was located. Seeing the motley group, Maharaj Shri said, "It is such a vast jungle. Why did you have to plan violence right before my eyes? I had to go out last night and free the suffering buffalo."

The Englishman visibly impressed by the royal-looking hermit said, "Please forgive me and my wife. Please help her if you can. I promise you that I shall never come here again for the sake of hunting."

"All right, all right, you may all go," said Maharaj Shri. As they turned round to go, they sensed that suddenly, miraculously, the lady was all right.

After a six-month stay at 'his' luxurious jungle estate, Maharaj Shri abandoned and rambled on to continue with his explorations. Once he was staying in a small village near the Rewa jungle. His ardent devotee, Kuberdutt Ojha, got scent of him and travelled all the way to the village. Maharaj Shri, who enjoyed giving his followers the full thrill of the chase, walked off into the jungle, as Kuberdutt arrived in the evening. Kuberdutt pursued him for two miles into the jungle, as night fell. Maharaj Shri stopped under a tree and spoke to Kuberdutt. He told him to sit and wait, excusing himself. Kuberdutt sat down a little grudgingly perhaps, and wondered why they had to leave the comfortable village and pass a hungry night in the darkness of the jungle. From somewhere appeared a man and handed him a small pot saying, "Please keep this, it's for you."

"Who are you? Where have you come from? What have you brought?"

"You just keep this," the stranger replied, "and give it to Maharaj Shri when he comes." Saying that, he left hurriedly.

Kuberdutt narrated the unusual happening to Maharaj Shri when he returned shortly. "Just see what is in the pot?" said Maharaj Shri in a matter-of-fact voice.

"It's full of fresh cream!" exclaimed Kuberdutt.

"Eat it to your heart's content and stop wondering who sent it. In future, just take what comes and no questions."

On another similar occasion, Maharaj Shri was sitting at night in a lonely place with a Brahmachari attendant when a man came and unpacked a sumptuous dinner for both of them. Seeing the curious look on Brahmachari's face, Maharaj Shri enquired about the sender's name and address. He made him note it down on paper. Next morning, he sent the Brahmachari to check up. It took him a long time to get his bearings, but finally he traced the village that he had noted down. And indeed there was a man by that name in the village. Did he send the stuff the previous night?

No!

* * *

A baffling man, Maharaj Shri. Here was one who needed nothing. Here was one who was complete in all respects, a whole man, a holy man. He possessed that, possessing which one possesses all. He knew that, knowing which one knows all. Yet, he was a man. To many he was an ordinary man. To many he seemed to have something extra. But to the discerning few, he was an extraordinary man.

Shri Gurudeva *with some*
disciples at Mussoorie.
Maharishi Mahesh Yogi is seen
at right.

CHAPTER SEVEN

Shankaracharya of Jyotirmath, Badrikashram

About fifteen hundred years ago, Shrimad Adi Shankaracharya had given a new dimension to the observance of Vedic religion. The knowledge of the Upanishads and the Bhagwad Gita came once again before the people in its crystalline form. It was the beginning of a new ethical era in the history of Indian civilization.

In order to ensure a continuous moral awakening of society, Acharya Shankar had set up four major Shankaracharya seats in four of the well-known Hindu centres of learning, situated in four parts of the Indian subcontinent. The northern seat of Jyotirmath had lain vacant for the last one hundred and sixty-five years, when in 1940 there was a move by the Indian religious federation, supported by many princely states, to find a suitable person to restore glory to this venerable seat. According to tradition it could be filled only by someone born in a chaste and renowned Brahmin family, someone linked by the Guru-disciple chain to one of the Shankaracharya Maths. He had to be a Dandi Swami who had entered the ascetic order in accordance with the traditional rites. He had to be learned, upright, intelligent, intellectual, well-versed in the Vedas, respecting the caste system and upholding the principle of Advaita or Cosmic Oneness. He had to be desireless and fully self-controlled, expert in propagating the techniques of yoga or union with the Divine. Such a one was indeed Maharaj Shri, now seventy years old. But would he agree to relinquish the quietitude that he loved so much and shoulder the responsibility of administering and restoring the pristine glory of the Shankaracharya institution?

When many people from many walks of life prevailed upon him, reluctantly he agreed to the proposal. Preparations were afoot for the investiture. Invitations were issued to delegates from all over India to come and attend the ceremonies at Varanasi, which were to form part of the deliberations of the Ninth All India Sanatan Dharma Sammelan.

But two days before the D-day, Maharaj Shri disappeared. Simply disappeared! Hoping, perhaps, that the big show would go on without him and that some other person would be instituted in his stead, he remained for many days in his hide-out.

There was a hue and cry over his vanishing trick. Rumours were set afloat. Some were in favour of appointing another person as Shankaracharya but Swami Gyanandji Maharaj, a respected leader, advocated a calm and unruffled appraisal of the situation and a postponement of the conference. Through a flurry of last-minute telegrams and trunk calls, the meet was adjourned indefinitely while a search began to locate the whereabouts of Maharaj Shri.

Twenty-one days later, Maharaj Shri of his own accord reappeared in Varanasi. The news of his arrival spread like wild fire and within an hour, at about 11 p.m., a group of erudite persons approached him and reiterated the request that he should accept the proposal of being the head of the Jyotirmath as he alone was capable of reviving the holy spirit of this Shankaracharya seat that had remained vacant for 165 years.

Shricharan remained silent, which was construed as consent. This time he was not asked to present himself for a formal investiture ceremony in the conference hall.

At sunrise on the first of April 1941, a small delegation of selected people headed by Swami Gyananandji Maharaj arrived at his Ashram. This Ashram, known as Brahmniwas, at Sidhigiribagh, Maharaj Shri had constructed five years earlier in memory of his Guru in whose name he had also formed the Shri 1008 Swami Krishnanand Saraswati Trust.

Maharaj Shri was anointed according to the prescribed rites. The ritual over, he was taken out in a grand procession to the venue of the conference where he was given a rousing reception amidst the sound of conch-shells and the chant of Vedic hymns. The Maharaja of Darbhanga State extolled Maharaj Shri and formally declared him as Shri Jyotishpeethodwarak Brahmleen Jagadguru Bhagwan Shankaracharya Shrimad Swami Brahmananda Saraswati-ji Maharaj, head of the re-established Jyotirmath, Badrikashram.

CHAPTER EIGHT

The Godman

Acharya Shri had two major jobs to do when he took over the charge. He had to reconstruct the institution and temple at Jyotirmath and he had to spread the Shankaracharya message far and wide. Specifically, he had to bring about a transcendental regeneration of Northern India. There were suggestions for collecting funds for this purpose in the big cities of Delhi, Bombay and Calcutta but he brushed them aside. He took over the entire responsibility for managing the finances himself and went about the whole thing in his own inimitable style.

He started with a triumphant tour of South India and on his return trip attended the Maharudra Yagya at Budhanpur in Madhya Pradesh. He was constantly on the move, receiving an enormous welcome wherever he went. Like a powerful magnet, he drew the multitudes to himself. His darshans were now very easy to obtain but they contained the risk of a lifelong attachment to him. Those who came under his aura became a part of his 'army'. They would ask him how best they could be of service to him and he would advise them to remain devoted to their respective Gurus and follow their teachings with sincerity and perseverance and to become disciplined and united participants in the Divine work.

He conducted numerous Chaturmasya Vrats at various places, made himself the centre of attraction at the Great Kumbh of Allahabad in January 1942. In Delhi he presided over the great Shatmukh Koti Homatmak Maha Yagya.

It was a memorable occasion when thousands of people had gathered on the banks of the Yamuna on a cold wintry morning to perform the requisite ceremonies. The rain-god also seemed eager to participate. The sky was overcast with thick black clouds. There was thunder and lightning and it looked as if it was a matter of minutes before it rained and hailed cats and dogs and camels and elephants. What a havoc would be wrought! Acharya Shri came out of his tent, looked at the sky and said quietly, "If it rains at this time it would cause a lot of disturbance," and went back to his tent. One hour later, the skyscape was altogether different. No clouds, a mild breeze, and sunshine!

It was a different story on his second visit to the institution base, Jyotishpeeth. The hill farmers around were stricken by the drought. It had not rained for three months. Even the sky remained cloudless. On the day Maharaj Shri arrived, there were clouds in the sky. Next day it rained, and it rained continuously for four days. We can guess the sort of welcome that he must have received from the simple peasants.

With the efforts of the organization that had nominated him, and the assistance of the Deputy Commissioner, Sir James Clay, Acharya Shri regained hold of the Jyotishpeeth land. Plans were drawn and the construction of the impressive double-storey building started. Materials such as paints, nails, bolts, knobs were not available there. They had to be obtained by post parcels at the expense of several thousand rupees. But the whole thing went through with consummate speed and very soon the Jyotishpeeth Bhavan with its thirty rooms was complete, and became a haven for pilgrims to stop on their way to Badrinarayan. They would also visit the beautiful temple of Purnagiri Devi, some distance away. The Darbhanga ruler had started construction of this temple shortly before his death. Acharya Shri had it completed.

With his extensive travels, his magnetic personality, and his lucid sermons based on experience, he was able to revive as it were the spirit of Shankaracharya in Northern India. There was an explanation for almost everything, even perhaps for his magical hold on his audiences. But wherefrom did he get the money to meet the lavish expenses that he incurred? He did not seek funds. He did not accept donations. In fact he had put up a signboard in Jyotishpeeth Bhavan that read, "Worthy of worship, Infinitely bestowed, Universal Guru Shankaracharya Jyotishpeethadheeshwar, Swami Brahmananda Saraswatiji Maharaj prohibits those coming for his darshan, pooja, deeksha, etc. to make any offerings of wealth." The title "Infinitely bestowed" given to him by his devotees had been used for the first time before a Shankaracharya's name as if it explained his unlimited financial adequacy.

There is an interesting incidence in this connection. In 1950, Acharya Shri was staying in Lucknow. Ruler of Daleepur State, Shri Pashupati Pratap Singh, had gone there for his darshan. One day the Raja proposed to him, "I have a mansion in Allahabad which I would like to donate to the Jyotirmath so that you have a Shankaracharya Ashram in that holy city."

Acharya Shri declined the offer. Reason: He did not accept donations. But when the Raja persisted with his offer, Acharya Shri agreed to purchase it in a regular manner and have the sale deed drawn in his name. He then called the Raja's secretary and asked him about the price. "Last year," the secretary said, "we had put up this property for sale and were demanding Rs. 100,000 for it but the highest offer we got was Rs. 65,000, so the deal did not materialize."

Acharya Shri thought perhaps that if he could get sixty-five thousand rupees from his hidden reserve, he might as well get a hundred thousand. Next day, he handed the money to the Raja of Daleepur and, on the latter's request, sent a man with him to Allahabad for getting the deed registered.

That was done. But it let loose quite a storm of whispers. How did Acharya Shri get hold of one lakh rupees when he never accepted donations and had no regular source of income? The registrar was asked, whether money was actually paid during the time of registration. Yes, he saw it with his own eyes. Were the notes real? Yes, they looked like real currency notes.

Two months later, Acharya Shri happened to visit Allahabad. People asked him, "Maharaj Shri, you do not accept money from anyone but you gave one lakh to the Raja. Where did it come from?"

"No human being was involved in this," was the cryptic reply. But it did not satisfy his listeners, who kept pestering him to resolve the mystery. So he tried, "During the time of the Mahabharat when the Kauravas unabashedly tried to strip Draupadi naked, where from did come yard upon yard of the saree that she was wearing. And it was of the same colour and design, thousands of yards. Not different colours. Not different designs. Same colour, same design, yard upon yard. When God gives, He gives all that is required: the whole thing—the real thing. What could take place at the time of the Mahabharat can take place now. God has not changed. He is beyond all change."

Acharya Shri modified, reconstructed and expanded the property that he had purchased. Consisting of many, many rooms and able to house hundreds of devotees, ascetics and Brahmacharis, it is known as "Brahma Nivas."

He stayed on for a month in Allahabad, then went to Varanasi. From Varanasi he went to Calcutta, where the Indian philosophical society was celebrating its golden jubilee. He had been asked to preside over the meet. Many philosophers, thinkers, intellectuals and social scientists had come from all over the world to attend the proceedings. Acharya Shri delivered a profound presidential address that won him a host of new admirers from among the distinguished gathering.

Next day, he was visited at 10 p.m. by Dr. Sarvapalli Radhakrishnan, one of India's most distinguished philosophers of modern times. With him were two well-known American philosophers Dr. Kangar and Dr. Shilpe. There was no appointment as such and Acharya Shri tried to put them off as was his wont but on his attendant's persuasion he acceded to meet them for a few minutes. They were ushered into his personal room, where they greeted him and sat down on the carpet. Introductions over, Dr. Radhakrishnan said, "Dr. Kangar would like to hear something from Maharaj Shri on Vedanta. He would like your assistance in experiencing the Truth-Essence."

Acharya Shri replied, "The Vedantic truth is self-evident and self-complete. It is Light itself. It needs no other light to illuminate it."

Dr. Kangar showing keen interest said, "But it cannot be said that the techniques mentioned in the Vedas to attain to the Supreme Essence are of no avail."

Acharya Shri clarified: "The techniques are not there to throw light on the Brahma-Essence. They are there just to dispel the darkness of ignorance, somewhat. They destroy ignorance by and by, but they do not illuminate Brahma. Brahma itself is illumination. No other light is required to illuminate it—just as the sun is self-illuminated and no other light is required to illuminate it. Before sunrise, the dawn dispels the darkness of the night, but does not illuminate the sun because the sun itself is illumination. All techniques are intended to destroy ignorance but they do not reveal the Innermost Self. The Self is Light, the Self is the Witness."

Highly impressed by this simple and lucid statement, Dr. Radhakrishnan and his friends bowed in reverence and took leave of Acharya Shri.

Acharya Shri was as much at home with men of reason as he was with men of blind faith, who deified him. He participated whole-heartedly in the pageantry loved by the common people. Invariably, he would be taken out in a procession passing through the main thoroughfares of the city. Arches would be constructed. The route would be decorated with flags and flowers. Almost everyone would turn out to have his darshan. Many devotees with big bowls containing sandalwood paste would move along the route applying it on the river of reverent foreheads on either side. He would inch along sitting in a decorated chariot that stopped every few yards. People would come forward, and garland him and worship him in the traditional style. There would be a continuous shower of petals from the precariously packed roofs and balconies of houses lining the route.

What did he think about all this *tamasha?* He made it clear many a time, as he once did to the citizens of Kanpur, "There was no need really to give me the sort of lavish welcome that you have just done. Yet Indian culture requires that the Guru should be given the highest respect and welcome, and therefore I do not object to all this fanfare and accept it. But there is yet a bigger welcome that all of you can give me. I have stepped down from the Himalayas and therefore deserve perhaps a Himalayan welcome. That welcome you can give me by giving me your time. That welcome you can give me by giving me your most valuable possession. What is your most valuable possession? Welcome me with that. My experience is that human beings value their vices above everything else. They are not prepared to part with them at any cost. Expense one does not consider. One is even prepared to suffer insult and injury for the satisfaction of one's most-prized vice. So make offerings of those vices to me. That is my service. That is my worship. That offering I willingly accept. In Kanpur there is a custom to make offerings in bags. But I am not one to be satisfied with offerings of rupees and paisas, which are like dust and pebbles to me. Offer to me bagfuls of your vices."

*   *   *

It was noon time, 4th December 1952, at 7 Canning Lane, New Delhi. The Indian President, Dr. Rajendra Prasad, had come for Acharya Shri's darshan. He paid his obeisance and listened to the Shankaracharya, who said, "In the olden days, rulers used to take advice from the sages in matters of state. With the wealth of their inner experience and purified intellect, they often came out with bold solutions to political problems. Their advice was untainted by selfish considerations and was given without fear or favour, and was generally one that benefited both the ruler and the ruled. The severance of this contact between Rajas and Maharishis has eroded the quality of administration and brought about discontent. Ethics and politics are not two separate entities. In fact, policies based on their integration are the most far-sighted policies and yield the best results. We always advise the citizens to live righteously and the more righteously they live, the easier is the job of the administrator."

The President listened to him with rapt attention. Touching on the subject of gurudom, Shankaracharya said, "The student does not set his own lessons. He needs a teacher to do it. For this reason to learn the art of well-being, the art of living a truly happy life, one needs an experienced Guru." He related some of his own experiences in this connection and added, "When I first met Guruji in Uttarkashi, my first request to him was, 'Please give me that knowledge which makes me self-sufficient so that I do not have to beg anything from anyone. Later on you can explain the Supreme Truth to me.' It is indeed my Guru's grace that till to-day I have never had to stretch my hands before anyone."

The meeting lasted half an hour more than the scheduled one hour. Only when Acharya Shri bade Dr. Rajendra Prasad to go, did the latter leave—may be somewhat reluctantly.

* * *

It was 20th May, 1953. Maharaj Shri was in his eighty-third year. The last twelve years as Shankaracharya of Jyotirmath had perhaps been his most strenuous ones, living constantly under the gaze of the public, travelling here, there and everywhere in India, coping with the milling crowds that thronged endlessly to have his darshan, to listen to his discourses and to worship the Divine Spark of which he was a very special manifestation.

He had not been keeping good health of late. Simple homeopathic medicines were being administered to him. Not finding them effective, allopathic treatment was being tried. Doctors called on him at 56 Balliganj, Circular Road, Calcutta. It was 1 p.m. on that fateful day. "Everything is all right," said the chief doctor. "His heart-beat is okay. The pulse is running well."

As the doctors left, he put his head down on the pillow, closed his eyes, looking very relaxed. Ten minutes later, he opened his eyes and said, "Help me to get up." Sitting up, he crossed his legs and closed his eyes in meditation.

At one-fifteen, he had gone—UP.

The news travelled through Calcutta like an electric current and then spread throughout India. People started pouring in an evergrowing stream. There was a spate of incoming trunk calls and telegrams. The All India Radio broadcast the news of the demise and announced that the body would be taken to Kashi for the final rites. His disciples, devotees and admirers, benumbed with grief, took what ever means of transport that were available and rushed to Kashi to pay their last homage to the great grand Guru.

There was not perhaps a single important town or city in India from which someone or the other did not wend his way to the Brahmanivas Ashram, Varanasi. They came from Lucknow and Kanpur, from Allahabad and Indore, from Jabalpur and Patna, from Katni and Ettawah, from Bombay and Nagpur, from Surat and Ambala, from Delhi and Agra, from Dehra Dun and Mussoorie, from Haridwar and Rishikesh, from Vishwanathpuri and Jyotirmath—a long line of mourners.

Maharaj Shri's body was placed on a truck in a seated position and taken to the Howrah railway station in a procession to the accompaniment of bells and conch-shells and music and hymns. The crowd on the route was so thick that it took more than three hours to get to the jampacked station. A specially decorated coach was connected to the Delhi Express which took off at 9.50 p.m. that mournful date. A group of devotees sang a rosary of devotional songs till the train reached Mughal Sarai around 3 a.m. Another hour by car and the scene was the Brahmanivas Ashram, Varanasi.

Tears flowed freely as one and all filed past his body, bowing before it and smothering it with flowers of love. Many stood speechless, unbelieving. His body was taken to his personal room and given a bath. A group of pandits recited verses from the Vedas. After the ritual worship, his body was seated on an artistically constructed *vimaan* which was placed atop a decorated truck.

The police band in front played *shehnai*, a mournful succession of notes on a joyous musical instrument. At the rear were singing and dancing groups 'celemourning' the departure from their midst of their beloved Master

Shri Swami Shantanand Saraswatiji Maharaj. *Present Shankaracharya of Jyotirmath.*

to meet the Lord in a final ecstatic embrace beyond the last vestige of physicality. A sea of people on all sides rippled slowly towards the time-honoured Dashwamegh Ghat on the banks of the Ganga.

The *vimaan* was lowered amidst the chant of appropriate Vedic mantras and placed on a king-size barge which moved slowly towards Kedareshwar Mahadev, escorted by a fleet of boats. On reaching Kedar Ghat, the mortal remains of the timeless one were transferred to a specially constructed heavy stone box placed in another boat. His *kamandalu* and *dand* were set beside the stately body and the coffin was shut. Then the boat oared towards the other bank. Alongside moved another boat equipped with gaslights that failed to dissipate the deathly darkness concealing the torrent of tears that mingled with the holy waters. When the boat reached the middle of the river, it stopped. The chest was lowered into the Ganga. Brahmachari Mahesh Yogi dived alongside and retained a touch of the precious container till it finally came to rest on the riverbed. Reverently, he bowed and surfaced again, sharing the agony perceptible in the faces surrounding him.

Five months earlier, Acharya Shri had executed a will and registered it with the District Registrar, Allahabad. That will was examined and given effect to by the Jyotirmath interim executive committee. At the auspicious time of 11.14 a.m. on 12th June, 1953, the successor indicated in the will was installed amidst great pomp and show. Shri Swami Shantanand Saraswatiji Maharaj, who commenced his tenure by offering puja to Maharaj Shri's sandals, has since kept aloft the flame of Shankaracharya which is but a subtle manifestation of the Supreme Light that has no end, that had no beginning.

**WHOLLY
IN
CONSONANCE
WITH
HUM
PLEASURE**